IMAGES
of America

NORWOOD

IMAGES
of America

NORWOOD

John M. Grove

ARCADIA

First published 1997
Copyright © John M. Grove, 1997

ISBN 0-7524-0848-8

Published by Arcadia Publishing,
an imprint of the Chalford Publishing Corporation,
One Washington Center, Dover, New Hampshire 03820.
Printed in Great Britain

Library of Congress Cataloging-in-Publication Data applied for

Contents

Acknowledgments

This work is the result of a collaborative effort made by a team of volunteers; all board members of the Norwood Historical Society. Without the vision, perseverance, and resourcefulness of these researchers and writers, this book would not have been possible. A sincere thank you is extended to Don Ackerman, Karen DeNapoli, Jean Detrick, Donna DiMarzo, and Maureen Graney—the team that produced this book.

Our appreciation for valuable assistance is extended to Ken McLean, John J. Cook, Bettina Cottrell, Bob Donahue, Ed Sweeney, and Denise Grove.

Thanks goes to Helen Abdallah, Catherine Connolly, Helen Donohue, Louise Drummey, Art Gearty, Phyllis Georgeu, Bea Grazado, Mrs. Thomas M. Hayden, Molly Hershman, Edwin Hubbard, Bart King, Elmer Marsh, Arline Veracka, Anne Sansone, Cindiellen Soderlund, Helen Soderlund, Ruth Very, and all those who came forward to offer their photographs and memories on Remember Norwood Day, April 13, 1997.

Special thanks to the board of governors of the Norwood Historical Society for allowing the photographs in the archives of the society's Norwood Collection to be available for this book as well as unlimited access to reference materials in the society's library.

All proceeds from the sale of this book will be used to benefit the Norwood Historical Society and for the preservation of the Fred Holland Day House.

Introduction

By the late seventeenth century, Sir Edmund Andros had made the journey from England to Boston to join his countrymen and to play a role in uniting the colonies, forming the Dominion of New England according to the royal plan. Around that time in nearby Dedham, town leaders were dealing with the problem of fellow citizen Ezra Morse and his mill. The waterpower required by Morse's mill was denying farmers downstream an adequate flow for watering their crops. The town needed both the mill and the crops, so the solution they found was to grant Morse another location for his mill. The wilderness known as the southerly part of Dedham was unpopulated and abundant with streams and timber—a perfect setting for the mill. Thus, the first European settlers moved into this forested area of the Massachusetts Bay Colony, a place which later became known as Norwood, Massachusetts.

The area was rapidly settled with citizens moving from Dedham village into the southerly part of Dedham, later to be formally known as South Dedham. Ezra Morse and his many descendants settled in the Morse Hill area in what came to be the neighborhood of South Norwood. The Dean family settled to the northeast on fertile farmland bordering today's U.S. Route 1, Dean, and Pleasant Streets. Everetts, Gays, Guilds, Haweses, Ellises, Days, Smiths, and Winslows all followed to this prosperous location. Each neighborhood within the area acquired an identity of its own. Today's Norwood Center was known as "the Hook," to the north nearer Dedham village was the Ellis neighborhood, and to the south nearer the town of Walpole was the Hawes neighborhood. Many knew the entire area as Tiot, an Native-American word meaning "place near the water."

In 1745, the British subjects living in South Dedham were well represented at the Siege of Louisburg. A memorial to the battle stands in Guild Square commemorating South Dedham's citizens who participated in this battle.

Although South Dedham is not the household word that Concord, Lexington, and Charlestown are to students of early American history, it was a vital thriving village in colonial America. All of the injustices inflicted upon the colonies by England were felt by the citizens of South Dedham. By the evening of April 19, 1775, residents of South Dedham had received word of the battles in Concord and Lexington between Redcoats and Patriots. According to legend, South Dedham yeoman Aaron Guild, upon hearing the battle news, dropped his plow in mid-furrow and left for Concord to assist his fellow Patriots. Today, the location is marked with a stone on the front lawn of Norwood's Morrill Memorial Library.

After the Revolution, the South Dedham community began to encounter more conflicts with the mother town of Dedham. Issues periodically surfaced around religion, schooling, and taxation. In 1828, the well-established Congregational Church was split. South Dedham parishioners founded a new Universalist Church using Paul Ellis' tavern at the Hook as a meeting place. A diverse community was taking shape, quite different from Dedham.

In 1849, the industrial age came to the village of South Dedham, with the arrival of the Norfolk County Railroad. This event has had a lasting affect on the community to the present day. The War between the States saw South Dedham's citizens in Union Army uniforms. South Dedham's tanneries were busy processing hides for boots, shoes, and gloves. By 1865, the town's population was 1,250; five years later it had increased to 1,560, and this prosperity soon attracted nineteenth-century entrepreneurs. The community had acquired a distinct personality by this time, and separation from Dedham was on everyone's mind. In 1872, this split became a reality, and Norwood was born.

During the last half of the nineteenth century, Norwood grew and the rural village evolved into a bustling town. With good rail connections, roads, and waterways, the area attracted industry from other New England towns. With these industries came the support services necessary for Norwood's workers and their families—blacksmiths, foundries, feed stores, and mills. The railroad continued to expand, with the Norwood car shops busy repairing and building locomotives and passenger cars.

The early twentieth century saw the development of the commercial business strip between Railroad Avenue and Guild Street, giving way to Norwood Center, the town common, and surrounding businesses. Residential building boomed north of Nahatan Street, along Railroad Avenue, and throughout neighborhoods known as Cork City, Dublin, the Ward, and South Norwood. In the mid-1930s, U.S. Route 1 bisected Norwood, and Nahatan Street was continued under the railroad tracks east toward Canton. This spurred the development of the area east of Norwood Center providing a location for the post-World War II residential building boom.

By 1907, the Norwood Historical Society had been formed to preserve the community's rich history. Many of the charter members were descendants of the original seventeenth-century settlers, most of whom had been present when the town was incorporated. Early society members were well aware of the importance of preserving the South Dedham/Norwood story for posterity. Today, society membership rolls include Everett, Morse, Guild, Dean, Morrill, and Winslow descendants, although members of these families are scattered all over the country. Residents of twentieth-century Norwood continue to pride themselves on their town roots. It is not unusual to find fourth and fifth generations of "townies" living in Norwood as their grandparents and great grandparents did.

The society archives are rich with photographs, wills, deeds, maps, business directories, and town records that are the sources for this book. Many of the images found here have never been published and are included to remind readers of how Norwood once looked and, more importantly, how it evolved.

As we close the twentieth century and observe the 125th anniversary of the town's founding, it is time to explore the rich historical heritage that surrounds us. Within our town's boundaries are treasures that provide a fabric for the town that deserve to be preserved and passed to our descendants as they were passed to us.

This work is not meant to be a comprehensive history of Norwood. Its purpose is to offer glimpses of our past in an attempt to make the reader aware that from a modern-day perspective, it is possible to peel back the layers of development and imagine, or in some cases find, the historical remnants that connect us to our collective past—not just Norwood's past, but the past of our nation.

One
Scenes of Old South Dedham

The Abijah Fisher farmhouse stood for more than one hundred years in a remote, undeveloped corner of South Dedham (Norwood) near Walpole's Bubbling Brook. The early-1800s homestead was bordered by neat stone walls and a small pond. "Pettee's Pond" powered Fisher's furniture mill and Percy Tisdale's sawmill. Nineteenth-century photographers often posed families standing outdoors in front of their homes. Pride of ownership and a sense of place are preserved in this *c.* 1870 photograph, although the house and barn were lost to fire fifty years later.

James Fairbanks built a handsome Greek Revival farmhouse in the late 1840s, on land deeded by his grandfather, Benjamin Fairbanks, and bounded by Prospect Street, a country road on a hill. An artful photographer captured a bucolic scene in the 1880s as a farm girl stood at the overlook. Today, the home's entries are enclosed. Land behind the house is replaced by a school parking lot, and the barn has been moved over and converted to a residence.

South Dedham's earliest families established farms on the fertile land of "Fowl Meadow" beside the Neponset River, as well as along Hawes Brook. Deacon Ebenezer Everett built a simple slope-roofed dwelling on the old Roebuck Road (Pleasant Street) in about 1740. Fred Holland Day, noted photographer and historian, documented the ancient relic, which remained at the corner of Willow Street in 1887. Known as Seth Everett's house, it was demolished before 1891. Day salvaged a fireplace crane and a cast-iron fire frame to use in the library of his father's remodeled home.

By the 1890s when Leonard Fisher was photographed standing in a jacket and overalls outside his early 1800s home on Neponset Street, Fisher families had lived for nearly two hundred years on farmlands bounded by Neponset, Pleasant, and Cross Streets. The house burned down, and today U.S. Route 1 cuts off the northerly end of Neponset Street.

The Dean Chickering house, built in the early 1800s, is an intact example of a stylish, hip-roofed Federal farmhouse. The central entrance pilasters frame a "fanlight" window. Missing today are the barn, stone walls, and granite fence posts setting off the front yard. Descended from Jabez Chickering, second minister of South Dedham's first church, this family owned extensive land to the west of their Walpole Street home. These farmlands, like those of their Guild and Everett neighbors, were broken up for development in the 1900s.

From the early 1700s, the Weatherbee and Ellis families occupied the northeast corner of what later became Norwood, below Clapboardtrees hill at the West Dedham (Westwood) line. Homesteads along the old Post Road to Providence (Centre Street, later named Washington Street) between Neponset and Everett Streets, came to be known as the Ellis neighborhood. David and Jabez Weatherbee lived in this early-1800s farmhouse on Neponset Street close to the corner of Washington Street.

In 1891, Peter Fisher purchased Caleb Ellis's c. 1853 house at Washington Street and Everett Street, opposite the old Ellis Railroad Station. Fisher ran a wholesale/retail florist business specializing in carnations. Remodeled in 1902, the simple home seen in this photograph sprouted elaborate additions. Allyn Fisher grew roses in heated greenhouses which stood behind the house until 1986, when condominiums were built on the site. The development was named Rose Court to reflect the property's history.

In the 1700s, Ellis Avenue was a cart road leading to the old Baker farm and Purgatory Swamp. In 1790, tavernkeeper John Ellis purchased the farm with its house and barns. The property passed to John Jr., Rufus, and Albert Ellis. Lost to twentieth-century development, a portion of its land along U.S. Route 1 is occupied by the Ellis Nursing Home today. This *c.* 1890 photograph captured a late-eighteenth-century relic, surrounded by a remarkably unspoiled rural landscape.

The *c.* 1822 Jesse Ellis farmhouse sits in restored condition on Ellis Avenue corner of Washington Street, opposite the Old Ellis Tavern site (demolished prior to 1860) and the Joel Ellis house. The two brothers' homes are the only remnants of a large farm at the center of the neighborhood. The last acreage was divided into house lots in the 1950s and 1960s. A dooryard fence and stone wall are seen in this *c.* 1880 photograph taken from behind a hitching post on Washington Street.

The Dean family came to South Dedham in the late 1600s. Their homesteads near the Neponset River formed an extended compound that grew to include six households by 1840. This early 1700s house on Pleasant Street just south of Dean Street descended to Thomas, then to Willard Dean. By the 1890s when this photograph was taken, the Morrill's Ink Works was located nearby.

Willard Dean's pantry, identified as the "cheese room" in a 1936 photograph, has the whitewashed beams and wide-board walls of a house very little changed from the 1700s. Except for the presence of a coffeemaker, the scene appears to be frozen in another time.

Willard Dean stood at the side doorway to his house in the 1930s, shortly before it was torn down. The entry enclosure was a mid-1800s "improvement" to his crude, one-and-one-half-story dwelling.

Cellar stairs in the old Willard Dean house were made of logs diagonally cut in half. Hand-hewn and pit-sawn beams and boards illustrate the structure of an early-eighteenth-century house. The photograph was taken in February 1936.

15

The historic Ebenezer Dean house stands today, a reminder of South Dedham's early Dean families and their descendants who farmed land bounded by the Road to Wrentham (Pleasant Street), the Road to Canton (Neponset Street), and the Neponset River. Built *c.* 1700 on a hill on the north side of Dean Street, it is the oldest house in Norwood. Its picturesque, sloping "saltbox" shape and center chimney are hallmarks of the first period in Colonial architecture.

On a hill west of Walpole Street near the corner of present-day Saunders Road was the home of Revolutionary War Captain Ebenezer Everett. His land extended westward to Oak Street and an area later called "Germany Plain" (renamed Westover in the twentieth century). Sold to Samuel Pond, the old house was an example of the simple saltbox-shaped structures typical in rural Massachusetts. George Harding Smith razed the house in 1898.

John Dean lived on 75 acres of farmland to the west of Ebenezer Dean's house, on a bend in Dean Street as it followed the Neponset River (west of modern U.S. Route 1). He was a nineteenth-century descendant of Deacon John Dean, one of the area's first settlers. The narrow windows of this wide, low structure look out onto a broad landscape. The sloped roof, with distinctive chimneys at its peak, identifies an eighteenth-century house, barely recognizable today in its much-modernized state.

In 1828, the Abel Everett Tavern was already old and in the way of development. Its site was chosen for a new Congregational church. According to local historian Win Everett, part of the tavern was rebuilt as the home of Lemuel Dean, after it was moved across Centre Street (now Washington Street near South Norwood), to the northeast corner of Chapel Street. Dean built a small grocery shop next to his house. "Lem Dean's" was known as South Dedham's first store. Neither building survives.

Deacon Willard Everett, born in the old Captain Ebenezer Everett house on Walpole Street, married Lucy Dean in 1821, and built this farmhouse and barn surrounded by apple orchards. He opened a furniture business after buying Jabez Boyden's cabinet shop. This was the start of the Everett Furniture Company, later moved to a central location in town and operated by generations of Willard Everett's descendants. Remodeled about 1860, the house stood until at least 1935 on the west side of Washington Street opposite East Hoyle Street.

In 1854, Josiah Tisdale opened a cobbler shop on the first floor of an old building on Nahatan Street, where he made and sold shoes and boots. Two apartments on the second floor housed his family and a brother. This photograph was taken after Josiah died in 1893, when the rooms were rented out to lodgers as "tenements."

In the 1840s, this was the residence of Charles Ellis, a c. 1800 farmhouse and barn set back from Walpole Street at its southerly end, just north of Ellis Pond. One of the stately elms on the property was known as the "5-mile" mark on the road from Dedham.

Raising fowl was a familiar part of an old-fashioned domestic life which persisted beyond the nineteenth century, even as the rural village became a suburban town. Standing in his henyard among the chickens and ducks, Isaac Ellis, farmer and retired ice merchant, displayed a prized hen for this c. 1890s photograph.

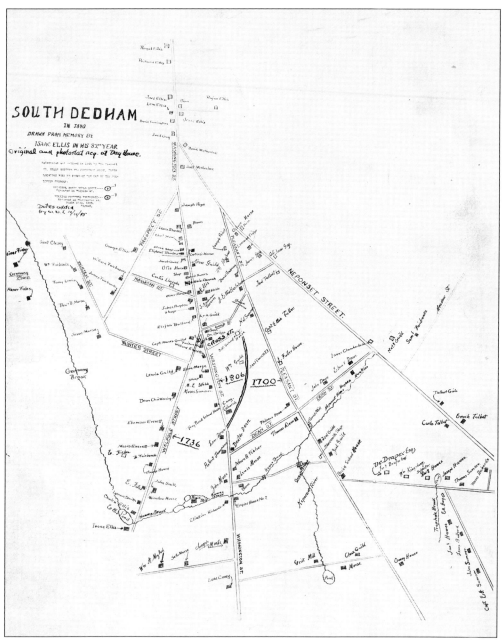

This map was drawn by Isaac Ellis in his eighty-second year. He laid out the roads and residences of 1840 South Dedham as he remembered them; for this reason it is not drawn to scale. Mr. Ellis lived at the southernmost end of Walpole Street, at the Norwood/Walpole boundary. As a patriarch of one of the area's oldest families, he must have known nearly everyone who lived in South Dedham before it became Norwood. In 1945 Win Everett added notes and corrections. Everett also was a descendant of early South Norwood settlers.

Two
The Hook

The heart of old Tiot was South Dedham's famous "Hook," an area at the center of town named for the iron hook in front of Paul Ellis' tavern, over which horsemen and coach drivers would throw their reins. To the left of Tinker's Drug Store was the second home of Caleb Ellis, with its lovely fence. In the center was a tavern, built for Paul Ellis in the early 1800s. This tavern was an important stop on the Norfolk and Bristol Turnpike and a local landmark until George Willett moved it in 1914 when he planned the construction of Norwood's modern town common. The large white house in the rear of this *c.* 1880 photograph was the former home of Paul Ellis, owned at that time by Joseph Day.

The west side of Washington Street between Cottage and Nahatan Streets is seen in a photograph dated to between 1886 when the Universalist Church (later reorganized as the United Church) was erected and 1896 when streetcars began to run down Washington Street. The brick commercial building mid-block is the Allen Talbot Building, built on the site of Talbot's house. Only the church pictured here remains at its original location.

This Italianate-style building formerly stood on the west side of Washington Street between Nahatan and Cottage Streets. In 1895, when this photograph was taken, Adams Express was located here. An undated advertisement refers to Adams Express, "forwarders of everything under the sun, dealers in choice groceries and houses to let."

The first Talbot Block in Norwood was one of Norwood's earliest brick commercial structures. It stood on the west side of Washington Street between Nahatan and Cottage Streets.

Village Hall was the site of Norwood's first town meeting in 1872. The building housed Masonic Hall, with Boyden's Grocery and Carter's Dry Goods at street level. When a new town common was created by George Willett, Cottage Street was extended across Washington Street and Village Hall was moved. The small building to the right in this *c.* 1900 photograph was James Folan's Boot Shoe Shop. The Folan Block was constructed in 1916 on this site.

On a sunny autumn day after the tall elm trees had lost their leaves, storefronts in the "Hook's" business district sported striped awnings. This photograph was taken from the foot of Vernon Street, before 1896. Looking north, behind Village Hall, was Tinker's Drug Store, where Norwood's first town clerk, Francis Tinker, kept offices.

This bird's-eye photograph of Washington Street looking south was meant to be viewed in a stereoscope. It was taken from the lower belfry of the Universalist Church (later reorganized and called the United Church). On the left are Village Hall and the First Baptist Church, which stood at the Washington and Vernon Street intersection.

William Fisher started his grocery business in this building in 1877. An old handpainted sign in the Norwood Historical Society Archives lists flour, tea, coffee, provisions, butter, hardware, and crockery among its offerings.

Joseph Day's early residence stood at the location of Norwood's Memorial Municipal Building (town hall). Day purchased the imposing Federal home of Paul Ellis, another prominent South Dedham businessman. It stood opposite Ellis' Tavern. To its right in this early-twentieth-century view is a temporary town hall, erected *c.* 1900 with a firehouse and tower. Considered unattractive, the hall was demolished after twenty-eight years.

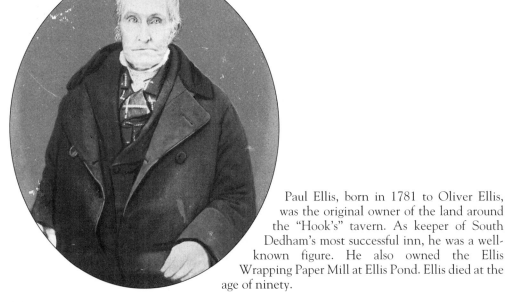

Paul Ellis, born in 1781 to Oliver Ellis, was the original owner of the land around the "Hook's" tavern. As keeper of South Dedham's most successful inn, he was a well-known figure. He also owned the Ellis Wrapping Paper Mill at Ellis Pond. Ellis died at the age of ninety.

Norwood House, with a wood-framed bandstand, was photographed by E. Altenbrandt in 1889. Known previously as the Norwood Hotel, it served as a public gathering place. Built by Paul Ellis and Lewis Rhoades in the first decade of the 1800s, the inn was operated by Ellis as an eating, drinking, and lodging establishment. He sold it to Joseph Sumner in 1828. Universalist Church founders persuaded Sumner to stop serving liquor, and he became a leader of the local Temperance movement.

Mrs. Sally Dudley Ellis was born in Cambridge in 1786 and married Paul Ellis in 1807. Their sons were Lewis, Paul Jr., Oliver, Charles, John, and Isaac. Sally passed away shortly after her husband died in 1871. Shown here in her old age, she had lived a hard-working and prosperous life.

27

Market Street in 1907 crossed through what later became the town common. It was discontinued in 1916 when Central Street was extended. The businesses on Market Street included Cornelius Horgan's Livery Stable, James Hartshorn's Market, Farnsworth Bakery, and Perley Thompson's Drug Store. Village Hall stood at its end on the corner of Washington Street.

This early street scene shows the businesses near the beginning of Market Street (formerly Cemetery Street). These buildings were dismantled or moved for the creation of Norwood's town common on this site. Note the early automobiles parked in front of the antique shop.

A brick firehouse was built *c*. 1907 on the corner of Nahatan and Market Streets (renamed Central Street). In the background is the Elijah Bullard house, moved to this location by Joseph Day. By the mid-1980s the former firehouse was remodeled to accommodate an upscale restaurant.

Mrs. Creed's Boot and Shoe Store stood at the beginning of Market Street adjacent to Village Hall in this *c*. 1895 photograph.

Built by Moses Guild, this eighteenth-century barn later became a steam-powered mill. Playing cards and shoes were made here before it became the carpentry shop of Tyler Thayer, South Dedham's foremost builder between the 1840s and the 1880s. It stood at the corner of Guild and Washington Streets until the early 1900s. Morrill Memorial Library, c. 1898, can be seen to its right.

Known as the "Old Corner House," this massive home stood at the northeast corner of Washington and Guild Streets until at least 1936. A major crossroads, the site is where Walpole Street meets Washington Street. Legend has it that the Marquis de Lafayette stayed here on his way to Boston in 1835.

Three
Roads and Railroads

Norwood's first ambulance appears in this early 1900s view, with its owner John Gillooly at the wheel. Founder of Gillooly's Funeral Home, he lived and practiced undertaking at 126 Walpole Street. This photograph was taken in front of George Metcalf's house next door. Norwood's 1911 Directory advertised Gillooly's "coaches, ambulances, hearses, and automobiles to let, office 605 Washington Street."

This 1890s view looking south toward Walpole on Washington Street in South Norwood shows the *c.* 1790 home of John Morse (eighth generation) and his son John's newer home. The older house no longer stands. In about 1812, after the road became part of the Norfolk and Bristol Turnpike, the Morses established a highway express service using the farmhouse's ample barns for relay teams of horses. Morse Express became the first stop for coach travel from Boston to Providence in the 1800s.

John Edwin Morse (ninth generation) was born in 1824 on his father's large farm in the southern part of South Dedham, a neighborhood settled by descendants of Ezra Morse. He took advantage of the property's location by launching the express transport company operated by his sons and grandsons until at least 1910.

After railroads came to South Dedham in the 1840s, John Edwin Morse and his father continued to operate a successful express business from a substantial new house and carriage barns built in 1853 (shown painted white c. 1890). Known for reliable transport, their chaises were entrusted to carry goods and valuables to Providence. They also delivered freight from railroad depots to local businesses.

In the twentieth century, the carriage barns were moved away and the John Edwin Morse house was painted in contrasting colors as it appears in 1997, highlighting its late-Victorian architectural features. This elegant home was built in the fashionable Italianate style of the 1850s with tall windows and quoin corner blocks. A long verandah faced the trolley tracks on Washington Street.

Norwood House was a hotel in the late 1890s when this parade passed by. Earlier in the 1800s, it was a tavern serving travelers on the Norfolk and Bristol Turnpike, an improved route between Boston and Providence. The toll road's construction began in 1802 and was completed through South Dedham in 1806. Now Washington Street, the road still marches through Norwood Center but is no longer a major highway. (This image also appears on the cover.)

A procession of horse-drawn carriages moved south on Washington Street through the business district in 1890. Its location on the turnpike road made the town's center very attractive to retail trade. Formerly Centre Street, this primary route from Dedham through Norwood was renamed Washington Street in the U.S. centennial year, 1876.

A horse and chaise travelling north on Washington Street was photographed in August 1886. Stacks of lumber filled the southeast corner lot of Tyler Thayer's carpentry shop. The Everett School was behind the shop and under an elm tree was a small building that served as the first water commissioner's office.

Workers laid tracks for the Norfolk Southern Street Railway on Walpole Street in 1899. This electric trolley line, later called the Norfolk and Bristol, operated for twenty years between Walpole and Norwood Center. Behind the construction crew is Chapel Street and Herbert Plimpton's mansion, later the headquarters of Norwood's Fraternal Order of Eagles. It burned in the 1970s.

This small wooden Central Station was more located the Original Norwood Central Picture station about 1900 or 1910, the New York and New England line This photograph was taken before 1899

A new Norwood Central Station was constructed on Central Street in 1899. Pictured about 1900 or 1910, the brick structure was restored and rededicated in 1992.

The crew of this freight engine was photographed as it stopped in Norwood. Of a type referred to as a "2-6-0" coal burning locomotive, it had two "pony" wheels in front, six driving wheels, and no trailing truck. The coal tender in its rear section was piled high. The crew included a fireman in the cab, three brakemen, and a conductor or engineer.

Winslow Station was located at Washington and Chapel Streets. It served an Islington-to-Blackstone, Rhode Island, line constructed in 1849 by the Norfolk County Railroad. During the 1890s when this picture was taken, the line was operated in turn by the New York and New England Railway; the New England; and the New York, New Haven and Hartford Company.

This granite railroad bridge over Dean Street in South Norwood dates from 1891. It was part of a 6-mile track extension completed in 1892 that extended from Walpole Junction through East Walpole to Norwood Junction and then linked up with the New York and New England railroad line near the Norwood Central Station. Today the extension is used only for freight trains.

Morrill's Station in South Norwood was a stop on the Walpole and Wrentham branch of the Old Colony Railroad (later the New York, New Haven and Hartford). It was built near Morrill's Ink Works in 1892, when industries sought to have railroad stations located near them. This 1890s photograph shows a coal bin to the right of the station and an Adams Express delivery wagon. Adams Express was a forerunner of railroad express companies that leased space on trains for shipment of goods and freight.

This New York and New England coal-burning locomotive was built in 1889. All New York and New England engines were frequent visitors to Norwood for routine heavy service and overhaul at the car shops near Norwood Central Station. The last remaining car shop, next to the Norwood Central Station parking lot, was demolished in June 1997.

During the 1890s, Norwood was served by five New York and New England Railroad stations. Proceeding south from Ellis Station near Westwood, Norwood Station was the next stop, followed by Norwood Center, Winslow's, and Morrill's Station. This is a *c.* 1900 view of the former Norwood Station at Railroad Avenue and Hill Street, with Fales Feed and Grain to its rear. The site is now known as Norwood Depot, a commuter rail stop.

Norfolk Southern Street Railroad tracks ran along Walpole Street in 1909, past John Ellis's house north of Ellis Pond. Built *c.* 1810 by John Smith, it was his son Lyman's home in the 1830s when John E. Smith and Anna Smith Day, two of Lyman Smith's three children, were born. Trolleys followed various local routes: from Walpole on this line (1899–1919); from East Walpole to Hyde Park on Washington Street (1896–1932); and from Canton over Neponset, Cross, Pleasant, Lenox, Broadway, and Day Streets (1900–1918).

Four
The Changing Streetscape

This view of Norwood Center from the top of Day Street is looking toward Washington Street, c. 1885. In the foreground is the old Bullard Farm orchard. The small-steepled church at the upper left is Columbia Hall, the original building for St. Catherine's of Siena Church. The larger-steepled church to its right is the old Universalist Church (later reorganized and called the United Church) that burned in 1884. In the center of the photograph, the Lyman Smith and Sons Tannery can be seen with Great Blue Hill in the background. The white house to the right of center is the Baker house, still standing in 1997 at the southeast corner of Bullard and Vernon Streets.

Joseph Day's residence, originally located on the northwest corner of Day Street and Washington Street, was built in 1855. Day purchased the Bullard farm from Elijah Bullard for $5,000. The farm was on the west side of Washington Street (then Centre Street), extending west to the present Day Street and Bullard Street area. Day was a wealthy leather merchant and an early real estate speculator. He can be seen here in 1872 with his wife, Hannah (seated on the lawn), and his daughter, Mary Cragin (on the veranda). Mary Cragin lived here until her death in 1888. Subsequent to its use as a residence, the home was also used as a parsonage for the Universalist Church and an office building until 1915, when it was sold to George F. Willet and moved west on Day Street (where it stands in 1997).

The original Day house at 93 Day Street was built in 1859 by architect B.F. Dwight and builder Tyler Thayer in the Mansard style for Joseph Day's son Lewis and his wife, Anna Smith Day. It was a near duplicate to the house built for Charles Smith (Anna's brother) at 108 Vernon Street. Lewis Day amassed his fortune in the leather industry. Anna and her son Fred can be seen here in front of the original home c. 1870.

Fred Holland Day, Lewis and Anna Day's only son, was greatly influenced by the English Tudor-style manor homes he saw on his travels in England. In the early 1890s he rebuilt the original Day homestead from the ground up to resemble his idea of the perfect home.

Every nook of this three-story, seventeen-room mansion reflects the influence of Fred Holland Day, a man who had left his mark on the world of art, publishing, and most of all, photography. The original 1859 carriage house can be seen in this 1976 photograph. The substantial remodeling of the 1890s did not include the carriage house, which was demolished in 1991. The Norwood Historical Society has called the elegant mansion home since 1934, when it was acquired through funds bequeathed to the society by Fred Holland Day and generous donations by society members.

The Elijah Bullard house was originally located at the northwest corner of Day and Washington Streets. When Joseph Day bought the Bullard farm, the farmhouse was moved to the corner of Lyman Place and Market Street (later known as Central Street) in the mid-1850s. This photograph *c.* 1930 shows the house before it was demolished to make way for commercial construction on Central Street.

Charles T. Wheelock built this Italianate Stick-style home on his father's 5-acre estate which had been purchased from Joseph Day in 1875. The house remains essentially intact today on the northwest corner of Maple and Cottage Streets. Charles Wheelock was a dealer of bookbinding materials and a candidate for town treasurer.

In 1855, the Lyman Smith house was part of the quartet of Italianate-style houses on the west side of Washington Street between Day and Cottage Streets. Architecturally, this house stands apart from the others, reflecting the success and lifestyle of its owner, Lyman Smith, a prominent Norwood businessman and owner of one of the two major tanneries in the town. The house was moved in 1915 to a site at 15 Vernon Street to make way for the construction of the Oddfellows Building on the northwest corner of Washington and Vernon Streets.

The Baker-Ambrose house, an early Greek Revival-style house, was built in 1855 for Joel Baker, a wealthy real estate broker and philanthropist. It, too, was built on land originally owned by Ellijah Bullard. Joel Baker was a major contributor toward the construction of the First Baptist Church that was located directly across from this home. He sold the house in 1906 to Alfred Ambrose, founder of the *Norwood Messenger*. The house was moved shortly afterwards to 12 Vernon Street (where it stands in 1997) to make way for the Sanborn Block.

The Dexter house, still standing at 25 Beacon Street, was originally part of the F.M. Cragin estate, which extended along Bullard Street from Day Street to Winter Street. The lot was sold to Nellie Dexter, an artist. The house was sited on the corner lot at the top of what was called Beacon Hill. Built *c*. 1898 in the Queen Anne Revival style, its octagonal corner tower rises to the height of three stories and is crowned by a pyramidal roof with a copper finial. This grand home was built during Norwood's building boom to lure people of substantial means out to the country. Homes of this style were sold for $10,000 with all the conveniences such as hot water heaters, plumbing, and gas fittings.

This photograph shows Nellie Dexter, the artist who lived in the home above.

Dr. John K. Briggs was the village physician. He married a daughter of Reverend Jabez Chickering of the Congregational Church. In 1820 Briggs built this stately residence and medical office set back from the southeast corner of Washington and Winter Streets and bounded by East Hoyle Street. The home was purchased by George Everett, president of the Willard Everett Furniture Company. In the fall of 1906, George F. Willet bought the entire property for the Norwood Civic Association's recreational complex which was constructed during the years 1909 to 1913. In the 1980s, Winter Street was closed at Washington Street to allow for expansion of Norwood Hospital at this site.

The Winslow-Berwick house, c. 1870, was originally located on a great lawn facing Walpole Street and was one of the best examples of Italianate-Mansard style. It was built by the Winslow family adjacent to land known as Winslow Park, land bounded by Walpole, Chapel and Berwick Streets. It remained in the family until 1891, when it was sold to James Berwick, who was later responsible with George H. Smith for forming the Norwood Press. In the mid-1920s a portion of the house was separated and moved to a new location, creating two residences. In 1997, both residences remain as 17 and 25 Berwick Place.

This c. 1913 view of Norwood Center was taken from the roof of the Conger Block on the southeast corner of Washington Street and Railroad Avenue. Washington Street can be seen on the right looking south. Market Street can be seen in the center of the picture with the old town hall facing it. The "lock up" stands behind the town hall and the firehouse is to the left. The steeple of the First Baptist Church at Vernon and Washington Streets can be seen, as well as the tower of the Plimpton Press in the upper left.

This roof-top view of the Washington, Guild, and Walpole Streets intersection shows Norwood's second commercial building, named the Talbot Block, c. 1912. To the left of the Talbot Block is the Premier Theater (later renamed the Guild Theater) with its arched entrance. On the extreme right, the steeple of the Methodist church (later the Christian Scientist Church) can be seen. The Plimpton Press, in the background, was a sprawling business during this period.

The Washington Street underpass at Chapel Street was created *c.* 1897 to accommodate the old Winslow Station and to cut down on fatal pedestrian accidents. A state investigation recommended that overhead bridges or underpasses be constructed to eliminate this problem.

In 1927, expansion of residential districts, under the inspiration of George F. Willet, consisted of 1,000 acres known as "Westover." It was conceived to demonstrate beauty of design and artistic merit for families of ordinary means. Opposition to this development led by his brother-in-law, Frank Allen, slowed the progress of Westover. In 1954, outside business interests began the prolonged task of making Willet's dream a reality.

Bill Gillooly, Curtis Fisher, and Fred Hartshorn Sr. race their horse-drawn sleighs down lower Washington Street in the 1880s.

Five
Providers

Walter Readel and Albert Warren were two employees of James A. Hartshorn, who operated a slaughter house in Walpole with his father, and later operated a butcher route from East Walpole. In 1881, Hartshorn opened a store on Market Street. The business was later moved to 615 Washington Street, where he operated wagon routes to Canton, Westwood, East Walpole, and Norwood.

The Ellis Ice House was a familiar site on Ellis Pond. Paul Ellis began harvesting ice from the Ellis Pond in 1864. His sons, Isaac, Frank, Louis, and Ernest, extended the business throughout Norwood, West Dedham (Westwood), Walpole, and Roslindale. The ice was used for the dairy and meat businesses which flourished in Norwood and Dedham.

The Issac Ellis house was located on the south end of Walpole Street near Ellis Pond.

Fred Holland Day
1886

John Ellis dammed Bubbling Brook and used the water power to run a sawmill. A second mill was built *c.* 1816 by John or his son, Moses Ellis. Moses's daughter, Mary Ellis, married James B. Tisdale in 1837 and left the mill to their son, Percy Tisdale (born 1846). Percy kept the mill running until about 1900 when the bigger mills forced him out of business. The sawmill, the meadow property, and water rights were sold to Winslow Brothers & Smith Co. tannery. In the early twentieth century, George Willett dammed Bubbling Brook further downstream which flooded the meadow forming the present Willett Pond (also known as New Pond). This water supply was used for the wool-pulling plant of the Winslow Brothers & Smith Co. This photograph was taken by Fred Holland Day in 1886.

This photograph shows lumber being transported by wagon from the Tisdale Saw Mill.

Established in 1853, Edgar L. and Erwin Bigelow were successors to L.W. Bigelow & Sons, purveyors of dry goods, gents' furnishings, and appliances. Located in Village Hall, a delivery sleigh was used to make local deliveries.

The Balfour Brothers Bakery, located at 658 Washington Street, was established c. 1900 by James, Margaret, Thomas, and William Balfour.

The Bigelow-Lepper house located at 25 Beech Street was built between 1889 and 1890. In the early part of the twentieth century it was owned by Erwin Bigelow of L.W. Bigelow & Sons and later, in 1920, George Lepper owned the house.

Alex Lepper founded a bicycle dealership in 1888 at Railroad Avenue and Washington Street adjoining J.W. Roby's Blacksmith Shop. The 1893 Norwood Directory reads "Alex Lepper Practical Machinist of 30 years' experience." George Lepper assumed control of the business and also became adept at repairing bicycles. In the 1920s, Lepper owned a Ford dealership at 579 Washington Street.

Alfred T. Harriott was a watchmaker, jeweler, engraver, and ophthalmologist. His business, established in 1881, was located at the intersection of Washington, Market, and Cottage Streets. To the right in this photograph is the post office where in 1897 William Wallace was the postmaster. On the second floor is the Thomas E. Clary Insurance Company where F.A. Morrill joined the firm in 1894.

Andrea DiMarzo is shown here with his wife Josephine and his sons Alfred, Charles, and Joe. DiMarzo was a master tailor with Hart, Schaffner and Marx until he moved to Norwood in the early 1900s and opened his own tailoring business on Washington Street in South Norwood.

The post office staff in 1903 consisted of, from left to right, Eva Hutchins, Anne Ellis, Frieda Formean, and Postmaster William Wallace.

From 1916 to 1935, the Norwood Post Office was located in the Norwood Associates block on Washington Street.

The Frank Fales house, located on the northwest corner of Nichols and Winter Streets, remains in 1997 at its original location. However, the barn seen in this photograph is no longer standing.

The Honorable Frank A. Fales was one of the civic pioneers of early Norwood. He purchased the flour, feed, and grain business of William Fisher in 1877 and in 1880 built the establishment on Railroad Avenue, which remained in operation until it burned in 1931. In 1882 Fales was elected to the board of selectmen. He also served on the first board of fire engineers, in the House of Representatives, the state legislature, and the state senate. He was the appointed postmaster of Norwood for twelve years.

Here is a portrait of local sawmill owner Francis (Frank) Morse (1821–1885).

Ezra Morse, from Dedham Village, was the first settler from Dedham to settle in South Dedham. His sawmill, established c. 1678 and located in what later became South Norwood, was South Dedham's first industry. His descendant, Francis Morse, whose house is to the right in this picture, established a sawmill in the late 1800s. The sawmill was located on Water Street near the East Walpole line. Remnants of this mill can be seen today where the Neponset River flows under the pedestrian footbridge on abandoned Water Street.

Clark's Pharmacy was located at 500 Washington Street on the north end of the Conger Block. Established *c*. 1900, this beautiful ornamental soda fountain was the last of its kind in Norwood. Shown here are Madge Clark and her mother.

In 1900, H.E. Rice & Company was "where you will always find an up-to-date assortment of dry goods, men's furnishings, fancy goods, and ladies' furnishings." Extending from 502 to 508 Washington Street, this shop occupied most of the Conger Block.

The Hawkins Block at the southeast corner of East Hoyle and Washington Streets was built by James Hawkins of Hyde Park between 1898 and 1900. It was later sold to H. Babcock, then to Mrs. Carberry. At 852 Washington Street, James Wellington was the "Prescription Pharmacist" at the Norwood Pharmacy in 1909.

Adolphus Holton's apothecary was located on Washington Street at the corner of Market Street c. 1897. Holton was also a photographer and a dealer in photographic materials and supplies.

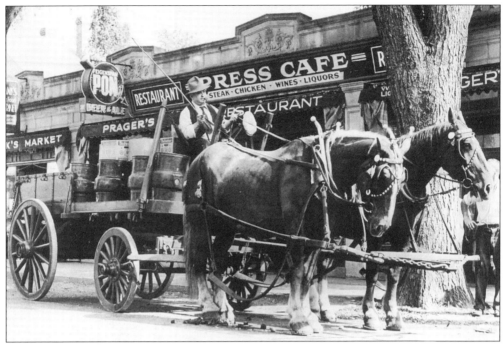

Nicholas Abdallah is shown here making deliveries by wagon from Nick's Package Store in South Norwood. Nicholas came to Norwood in 1912 with his father John, who established the South End Hardware Company at 1043 Washington Street. He is the father of John Alec Abdallah, who served as a Norwood Selectman from 1956 to 1968 and for whom the Neponset Street bridge over Interstate 95 is named. The Balch School Addition is named for this civic-minded individual.

In 1874, Milton H. Howard was an established contractor and master builder in Norwood. Among his numerous works are the Universalist Church (later reorganized and called the United Church) and many of Norwood's early school buildings. Howard succeeded Tyler Thayer as the foremost builder in Norwood. He was the first president of the Norwood Historical Society.

Six
Captains of Industry

South Dedham's tanneries provided the raw material for gloves, boots, and hats, which supplied the Union Army in the War between the States. Tannery operations in the town provided lifetime employment for hundreds of residents from the early eighteenth century well into the twentieth century. In this late-nineteenth-century photograph taken at Winslow Tannery on Endicott Street, future Massachusetts Governor Frank G. Allen can be seen (back row, first from the left). Allen eventually went on to run the tannery after marrying F.O. Winslow's daughter, Clara.

The tanning industry and the Smith family of South Dedham were synonymous throughout the nineteenth century. John Smith, pictured with his wife Anna, was the patriarch to three generations of tanners in South Dedham/Norwood, starting an industry that prospered in the area for almost two hundred years.

South Dedham's first tannery can trace its roots to Abner Guild in 1791. Guild apprenticed young John Smith in the tanning business. Smith in turn mentored George Winslow, who came to South Dedham in 1826. Winslow married Smith's daughter Olive, and a strong family and business partnership was formed as this tannery on Endicott Street (pictured here) became the Smith and Winslow Tannery. In 1853, the partnership amicably dissolved and the tannery on Endicott Street reverted to the George Winslow and Sons Tannery while John Smith's son Lyman built a new tannery north, on Railroad Avenue nearer to the "Hook." In 1901, the tanneries combined again as Winslow Bros. and Smith Co.

After a separation from South Dedham's original tannery founded by the Winslow family, Lyman Smith and his sons, John and Charles, began this tannery operation on Railroad Avenue between Hill Street and Cemetery Way (later renamed Central Street).

Workers at the Winslow tannery pause in their work clothes, tools-in-hand, for this photograph outside the tannery on Endicott Street.

In July 1858, John E. Smith began to buy small parcels of land between Day and Winter Streets ultimately acquiring 12 acres. He built his home on the western boundary of these 12 acres at Beech and Day Street. At that time, it was the only structure on the land that eventually saw the construction of Morrill Memorial Library, the Beacon School (original high school), the fourth site of the First Congregational Church and parsonage, and homes of other prominent townspeople.

John E. Smith is seen seated in the well-appointed parlor of his magnificent home after a substantial remodeling in the early 1890s.

Willard Everett started a small cabinet shop known as Willard Everett & Company. By 1865, the Everett Furniture Mill was located on the west side of Broadway opposite Norwood Central railroad station. The mill was operated by George and Frank Everett, who employed over 150 men crafting fine furniture and shipping it all over the United States, Cuba, and the West Indies. The cabinet shop is credited with making the first extension tables in America. The mill was totally destroyed by fire in May 1865, and never rebuilt. The craftsman found jobs in Boston furniture-making businesses, and one of South Dedham's earliest industries vanished from the area.

South Dedham, *Apr 4* *1853*

Mr Thos. B. Dean

Bought of WILLARD EVERETT & CO.,

WHOLESALE TABLE MANUFACTURERS.

Cherry and Black Walnut Extension Tables, Common do., Grecian, Saloon, Reading, Toilet Tables, Washstands, Tea Poys, &c., made to order, and in the best possible manner.

To Sub Butter from C. C. Barnes. *$10,00*

Rec. Payment

Willard Everett & Co.

In 1892, the Norwood Business Association was organized with the intent of attracting new business to the growing community. The association raised money to acquire the land that led, in 1894, to the founding of Norwood's prosperous book printing industry. Three independent companies, the J.S. Cushing Co., the C.B. Fleming Bindery, and Berwick & Smith, consolidated their operations in Norwood to become the Norwood Press. Specializing in rapid turn-around, the Norwood Press gained a worldwide reputation for quality among publishing companies. The Norwood Press printed high school and college textbooks and bibles in the early part of the twentieth century. In contrast to the tannery and railroad industries, book printing was considered a more up-to-date industry for early-twentieth-century Norwood.

Norwood Press workers gather outside the press buildings located at Walnut and Washington Streets for this photograph, taken in the 1890s.

Workers of the Norwood Press posed for this *c.* 1900 photograph on the loading dock.

Two men demonstrate the inking process outside the Norwood Press building.

This is a portrait of George Harding Smith, co-founder of Berwick & Smith, one of the partners in the group that formed the Norwood Press.

George Harding Smith resided in this home on Walpole Street at Saunders Road. The front lawn of this property originally fronted on Walpole Street. The site was formerly occupied by Ebenezer Everett's home. During the 1898 construction of Smith's home, a granite mile marker was unearthed inscribed with "1740 Boston Townhouse 14 miles E. Everett." Smith valued the granite marker and saw to it in his will that when the home was no longer occupied by his family, the granite marker would be donated to the Norwood Historical Society. In 1929, the home was sold by Smith's descendants and it was converted into a home for the aged. Much-altered since 1929, what remains of the home can still be seen in 1997, as an assisted-living facility.

J. Stearns Cushing posed with his daughter Lilias at the Saunders Road gate of their home.

J. Stearns Cushing, one of the magnates of the Norwood Press, lived in this Colonial Revival home on Highland Street at Saunders Road. The home, built c. 1905, was considered one of Norwood's most lavishly detailed mansions and was praised as an ornament to the town. This elegant property was demolished for the development of homes on this site in late 1996.

In 1897, Herbert M. Plimpton joined the Norwood Press in establishing the printing industry in Norwood. The firm, located on Plimpton Avenue at Lenox Street, continued increasing printing capacity at that site through the 1950s.

This March 1915 interior photograph of the Plimpton Press's accounting department shows bookkeepers and clerks using up-to-date mechanical calculators and typewriters. Note the window-frame-mounted electric fans used for summertime ventilation.

Plimpton's Queen Anne-style Norwood home was located on Chapel Street at Walpole Street, as shown in this early-twentieth-century photograph. To the rear can be seen one of George Winslow's homes.

Workers pause at the Plimpton Press for this 1906 photograph taken among unbound book pages.

In the mid-1850s, Samuel Morrill and his two sons, George H. and Samuel Jr., moved their prosperous ink production business from Andover, Massachusetts, where it was founded in 1840, to South Dedham. The location on Pleasant Street south of Dean Street grew to include fourteen buildings by 1884. By 1913, it was the largest ink works in the world. In 1929, it became part of the Dillon Read Company, although it retained its Morrill identity. In the 1970s under the auspices of Sun Chemical Corporation, the ink works ceased operations in Norwood.

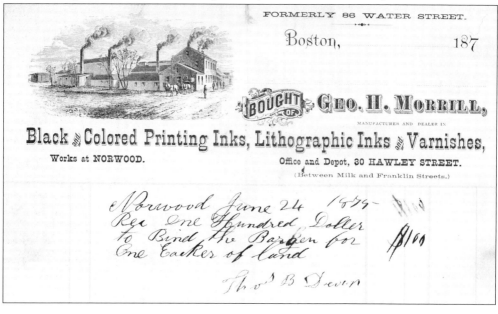

George H. Morrill Sr. and his second wife, Louise J. Tidd, made their original South Dedham home on Dean Street within sight of their ink works on Pleasant Street.

With the success of the Morrill Ink Mill George and Louise Morrill built a home more fitting their position in the community. This home located on Nichols Street passed from the Morrills to Norwood merchant H.E. Rice. Although it has been substantially remodeled and relocated, it can be seen in 1997 at 137 Nichols Street serving as an assisted-living facility.

George H. Morrill Jr. called his home the Pines. It was magnificently sited at Bond and Nichols Streets. It was demolished to make way for other residences. Bond and Morrill Streets now traverse what was the original site. Tradition has it that George Morrill had the first gasoline-powered carriage in Norwood.

Edmund J. Shattuck, his wife, Emma Louise Morrill, and their five children resided in this fine home on the southwest corner of Walpole and Winter Streets. Emma was the daughter of George H. Morrill Sr. Born in Northfield, Vermont, Edmund came to Norwood in 1873. At the time of his death in 1903 Edmund was managing the George H. Morrill Co. He served as water commissioner for Norwood for fourteen years. Their daughter, Maud Shattuck, resided in the home until her death in 1962. Shortly thereafter, the home was demolished. Today, all that remains is the carriage house on the Bond Street side of the property, which serves as a social hall to the First Baptist Church.

Seven
Friends and Neighbors

Josiah Warren Talbot was nicknamed "Shout" after being struck by lightning as a child and losing his hearing in one ear. In 1860, Talbot bought the old Lewis Rhodes farm on Centre Street (Washington Street) where he researched pomology (apple breeding). He studied unusual subjects and popular sciences of the Victorian era, such as phrenology, a theory linking personality traits to head and skull characteristics. A respected teacher and minister, Talbot was chosen to present to the Massachusetts Legislature a petition for separating South Dedham from Dedham in 1872, thereby creating the town of Norwood.

This photograph of the Baker house can be dated to between 1859 (when the Lewis Day house, seen to the rear was built) and 1892 (when the Day house was remodeled in Tudor Revival style). The Baker residence was constructed in Italianate style by prominent builder Tyler Thayer for Francis Metcalf Baker, a successful expressman. It stands at 80 Vernon Street on the corner of Bullard Street.

A second-floor front chamber in the F.H. Baker home was fitted out in high Victorian style of the 1880s. Leaf-patterned wallpaper with floral borders, expensive wall-to-wall carpeting, and an oriental rug provide an elegant backdrop for a reclining sofa, a Gothic Revival chair, and an Eastlake table. The fireplace, draped with silk hangings, is topped with a French mantle clock. The photograph seems to invite the visitor to sit down, but to do so carefully.

Four generations of the Baker family posed for a photograph taken about 1865. Obed (on the left) was eighty-one years old. Joel Metcalf (1808–1878) contributed to the construction of the First Baptist Meetinghouse in South Dedham. Francis Metcalf, who died in 1898, was a deacon of the church for twenty-five years. William Francis was born in 1862 and died in 1924.

A neighborly group of men (William F. Baker at left, and Samuel and Nathaniel Reed) sit on a cesspool cover in grocer Ernest Grant's back yard at 171 Vernon Street. Behind them 135 Cottage Street can be seen surrounded by undeveloped lots. Soon after this c. 1898 photograph was taken, new homes lined both sides of Cottage Street.

Dr. Francis M. Cragin moved to South Dedham and set up a homeopathic medical office in 1868. He continued to practice here until his death in 1911. He married Mary E. Day, daughter of Joseph and Hannah Day.

Dr. Francis M. Cragin lived and practiced medicine in this house at the corner of Walpole and Beacon Streets. It was formerly the site of the Balch Parsonage, the early 1700s residence of South Dedham's first minister. The Beacon School, built in 1890, can be seen to the rear of the house in this photograph. On the left, behind the elm trees, is the fourth house of worship of the First Congregational Church, built *c*. 1884. The Cragin house is the only building in this 1890s photograph that remains in 1997.

An elegant Mansard-roofed home was built in the French Second Empire style by Tyler Thayer for Charles Lyman Smith, c. 1866. C.L. Smith, son of tannery industrialist Lyman Smith, ran the tannery along with his brother John. Smith's home is located on the corner of Vernon and Maple streets. It was later the home of Dr. F.S. Baston.

Ralph Metcalf Fogg, born in South Dedham in 1855, was a prominent Norwood dentist, with his home and office at 30 Walpole Street. The building is still extant in 1997. He also had offices in Boston, Dedham, and Quincy. Dr. Fogg was known for his invention of "Boston Vegetable Vapor," used by dentists around the country as an anesthetic.

The Perley Evans house (on the right) still stands on the southeast corner of Walpole and Winter Streets at 96 Winter Street. With its massive form and turret, it is a prime example of the Queen Anne style in Norwood. The houses along Winter Street, on the left toward Washington Street, were also built in the 1880s and 1890s.

Harriet Evans was a member of the Universalist Church and first chaplin of the Samoset Club. She lived in her home at 96 Winter Street until her death in 1926. Her husband, Perley, was an engineer employed on the New Haven Railway line.

Henrietta Doane, daughter of George Winslow, is shown inside her home at 269 Walpole Street on her ninetieth birthday (c. 1932). She enjoyed fine, comfortable furniture and a very grand birthday cake.

The house at 269 Walpole Street was built c. 1850 for George Winslow in the latter part of his career as a tannery industrialist. In 1860, he retired to this substantial Italianate house overlooking Winslow Park (now Disabled American Veterans Park), while his sons carried on the family business. George's only daughter, Henrietta, married Francis Doane, a stationer, in 1879, and the house was given to them as a wedding gift. It has changed little in appearance over the years.

In 1833, Curtis Morse bought a two-acre parcel of land on the southeast side of the turnpike road (now Washington Street). He built this picturesque Greek Revival cottage, elaborately fenced off from the street. Morse owned a cabinet shop in the Old Stone House across Washington Street, where he manufactured fine furniture. Only the Old Stone House remains in 1997. Later the furniture company moved to Railroad Avenue. It eventually relocated to Boston as Haley, Morse, and Boyden Furniture Company.

Curtis Morse and Fannie Boyden married in 1832. Curtis was a descendant of Ezra Morse, the first permanent settler of what is now Norwood. His wife was also a member of an old South Dedham family. An early daguerreotype, c. 1840, captured their expressions, hands, and details of their dress with exceptional clarity. Morse's plaid vest and jaunty neckcloth stand out in contrast to Fannie's sober portrait.

This grand Second Empire house was built by Tyler Thayer for E. Fisher Talbot in the 1860s. Talbot established a carpet factory on Railroad Avenue in 1853. A fire set by a disgruntled worker burned the business, along with Talbot's first home. Both were rebuilt in 1860. Talbot's bad luck continued when an accidental fire destroyed his second home and industry. Demoralized by his loss, he considered a move to Philadelphia, but his South Dedham neighbors rallied to build a new factory and residence for him on Washington Street land donated by his brother George. E.F. Talbot died in 1882. His last home still stands in 1997 at 465 Washington Street, its impressive Victorian details hidden behind synthetic siding.

The house at 314 Nahatan Street (seen to the left) had a third-floor turret room added to its front bay after this photograph was taken. Lucius White, son of nationally recognized grape breeder Nelson B. White, lived here at the turn of the century. Norwood's best surviving example of a Carpenter Gothic cottage is seen to the right at 317 Nahatan Street with steeply pitched gables and carved wooden trim. Except for aluminum siding, it is little changed from its appearance in this 1890s photograph.

Frank G. Allen posed with his eldest daughter, Mary, about 1903. Allen was born in Lynn in 1874, the son of a tannery worker. At age twenty-two he came to Norwood, working his way up to become chairman of the board at the Winslow Brothers and Smith Tannery. He contributed to the local funds and charities, particularly Norwood Hospital, and was a town selectman. After two terms in the state senate, he served as governor of Massachusetts from 1928 to 1930. Allen resided in Norwood for forty-eight years, until 1944.

This Shingle-style home with Colonial Revival porch columns was built c. 1909 by architect Milton H. Howard for Frank G. Allen. One of several distinguished residences built west of Walpole Street for early-twentieth-century businessmen and civic leaders, it stands in nearly original condition, set back from Fisher Street on spacious grounds. In 1913 Allen, along with his wife, Clara, and daughter Mary, moved to the mansion of his father-in-law, F.O. Winslow, at 289 Walpole Street.

George H. Morse built this Italianate house and barn in 1868, atop Morse Hill near the South Norwood/East Walpole line. He was a descendant of the area's first settler, Ezra Morse, whose ancient saltbox-shaped dwelling on this hill was torn down in 1865. Thus, George Morse's home has been known as the site of the first house in South Dedham. An auctioneer and appraiser in 1884, at about the time this photograph was taken, Morse also served as a town selectman.

George H. and Althina Atkins Morse had their portraits taken at a Boston photographer's studio. Mounted on pressed cardboard, these cartes-de-visite were handed out to friends. Like calling cards, they were social prerequisites in the late nineteenth century.

In 1909, W. Curtis Fisher and Emily Atkins Fisher posed under a bridal arch arranged over the entrance to their family homestead at 345 Neponset Street, while the Norwood Band played on the lawn. The happy occasion was their fiftieth wedding anniversary. Mr. Fisher was a fifth-generation farmer.

In the 1884 Norwood Directory, Thomas O. Metcalf advertised a printing business in Boston which also manufactured tags for shipping, merchandising, and jewelry. Today the Metcalf house at 120 Walpole Street looks very much like it did when this *c.* 1881 photograph was taken, but the open landscape around it has filled in with dense residential settlement.

Men and women at the turn of the century stand around a boarding house located on the west side of Washington Street across from the Norwood Press. A sign on the porch railing reads, "BOARD BY DAY OR WEEK."

Oakview is Norwood's finest example of the Second Empire Mansard style of architecture. The Walpole Street home was built in 1868 for Francis Olney Winslow, an heir to a fortune derived from the tannery business begun by his father, George Winslow.

Friends and neighbors often referred to F.O. Winslow as "Mr. Norwood." He was a leader in business, investments, civic affairs, town government, state politics, philanthropy, education, history, and the arts. In 1866 he married Martha Robie. Their two daughters, Clara and Edith, both married men who became prominent in town and state government, Frank G. Allen and George F. Willett respectively.

Norwood milliner and banker Walter F. Tilton built this home *c.* 1901 on Beech Street near the corner of Winter Street. It has since been moved slightly away from Winter Street and back from Beech Street on its original lot. Tilton followed the lead of the Morrill and Day families by bestowing a lasting gift upon the town; the fifty-bell carillon in the town hall's tower was donated by Tilton in 1927.

Walter F. Tilton was an important figure in the early years of Norwood. He was a founding member of the board of directors of Norwood's first bank, the Norwood National Bank. He was also one of the founders of Norwood Hospital and one of its major benefactors. Mr. Tilton died in his home at 49 Beech Street in 1950 at ninety-three years of age.

Four generations of Norwood's Morrill and Shattuck women were photographed together. Mrs. George H. Morrill Sr., Mrs. Edmund J. Shattuck (Emma L. Morrill), and Mrs. W.W. Adams Jr. (Louise Shattuck) passed along their strong family ties to baby Janet Adams.

Mary Day and Anna Smith were close neighbors on Centre Street. Anna lived with her father, Lyman Smith, on the corner of Vernon Street. Mary lived with her father, Joseph Day, on the corner of Day Street. Centre Street was later renamed Washington Street and both of their homes were moved slightly west of Washington Street. This daguerreotype was taken about 1853. Anna Smith later married Mary's older brother, Lewis Day.

Eight
Schools and Churches

Norwood's first high school, located on Beacon Street, opened in the spring of 1890. In 1898 the Morrill Memorial Library occupied the site between the school and Walpole Street. It was later enlarged and called the Beacon School and was used as a lower grade school after completion of a new Norwood High School on Washington at Bond Street. The Beacon School was demolished in 1942.

In 1893, the students of the Beacon School posed for this picture.

Abbie White's public grammar school and class was photographed in this picture dating from 1879. Begun in 1873, the school was located at the northeast corner of Washington Street and Railroad Avenue. It was razed in 1929 to make way for a gas station.

In 1898, the students of the West School gathered for their picture. Ella Gates was the teacher.

The West School stood on the southwest corner of Walpole and Eliot Streets. Built in 1891, this two-room building was in use until 1907, when it was declared inadequate. It reopened in 1911 to relieve congestion at the Winslow and Guild Schools. In later years it housed the administrative offices of the Norwood Public Schools and is now a professional building.

This was a first grade class at the Guild School in 1893. In the background you can see the teacher, Orra Guild.

The Guild School, built in 1894, was located on the west side of Central Street near Guild Street. The school was destroyed by fire in 1929.

The Everett School was built in 1851 and was located on Central Street near the present site of the post office, which was built in 1935.

Students at the Everett School were photographed in 1885.

The earliest record of the "Old Brick School" can be found in documents dated 1788. Located at the intersection of Pleasant and Sumner Streets, this building was built c. 1800. It was last used as a school in 1866. In 1867, the Balch School was opened on Washington Street to replace the "Old Brick School." The building, threatened by commercial development, remains standing in 1997.

The Balch School as it looked when built in 1867. It was named after Reverend Thomas Balch, the first minister to the village of South Dedham. The present-day Balch School occupies the same site.

The combined faculties of the Everett and Guild Schools posed for this picture in the spring of 1897.

The third house of worship of the First Congregational Church was built in 1828 and was located on Washington Street near Chapel Street.

The fourth house of worship of the First Congregational Church was dedicated in 1884 and located near the corner of Winter and Walpole Streets. The parish house was located to the north near Morrill Memorial Library. In 1997, a medical building occupies the site.

Reverend Arthur H. Pingree (1867–1915) became pastor of the First Congregational Church in 1902. He married Juliette Christie Merrill, daughter of the headmaster of Boston Latin School, in 1903. A founder of the Boy Scouts and Camp Fire Girls in Norwood, he ran a summer camp on the Annisquam River at Pigeon Cove in Gloucester. On July 19, 1915, Reverend Pingree drowned while trying to save two girls caught in the river's current (one survived). He was posthumously awarded the Carnegie Medal for Heroism.

Hannah Balch Chickering (1755–1839) was the daughter of Reverend Thomas Balch, the first pastor of the First Congregational Church. She married Jabez Chickering, the second pastor of the church, on April 22, 1777.

The Balch Parsonage stood on the present site of 17 Walpole Street. Built in 1736 by Reverend Thomas Balch next to the First Congregational Church on the busy post road between Boston and New York, it became the social center of the community. It was eventually moved to Broadway and later demolished.

This is the second church building of the Universalist Church. It was destroyed by fire in 1884. It was rebuilt and dedicated in 1885 at the southwest corner of Nahatan and Washington Streets, where it remains in 1997 as the United Church.

Columbia Hall, originally the First Universalist Church, was later used as a Catholic church and dedicated as St. Catherine of Siena Church in 1863. It was located on the present site of St. Catherine's Rectory on the west side of Washington Street between Nahatan Street and Railroad Avenue.

The First Baptist Church and Parsonage was dedicated in 1859 and was located in the Washington Street business district across from Vernon Street. This original wooden Italianate building was torn down in 1950, and the congregation moved into its present building at the corner of Walpole and Bond Streets.

The hurricane of 1938 did considerable damage to Norwood's First Baptist Church, then located on Washington Street. The replacement steeple erected as a result of this damage forever altered the appearance of the church.

The chapel of St. Gabriel the Archangel at Highland Cemetery was erected by Lewis and Anna Day to the memory of their parents, Joseph and Hannah Rhoades Day and Lyman and Melinda Guild Smith. The chapel was consecrated and donated to Norwood on Memorial Day, 1903.

Cram, Goodhue, and Ferguson of Boston, the leading ecclesiastical architectural firm of the day, designed the Chapel of St. Gabriel the Archangel. This interior view of the chapel shows the altar, bier, and the separate chantry on the left where Lewis and Anna Day are entombed.

Nine
Building a
Twentieth-Century Town

The ground-breaking ceremony for the new municipal building took place in 1927. Dignitaries gathered to officially start construction on the limestone structure that completed the physical identity of Norwood Center.

This nighttime photograph of the Norwood Town Hall was taken on November 10, 1928. The building was formally dedicated the next day as the Norwood Memorial Municipal Building.

The Folan Block, named after Joseph M. Folan, was constructed in 1916 and located on the southeast corner of East Cottage and Washington Streets. The site was previously occupied by South Dedham's Village Hall, which was moved to Broadway to accommodate construction of commercial blocks in the growing town's center.

The State Armory at Norwood was dedicated in January 1930. Then-Governor Frank G. Allen, from Norwood, pressed for the state to build the armory in Norwood and was present at the groundbreaking and dedication. The Commonwealth of Massachusetts sold the armory to the Town of Norwood for $1 in 1984. It was rededicated as the Norwood Civic Recreation Center, the namesake to the "Old Civic" which had been located on Washington Street at East Hoyle Street.

By 1929, George Willett's vision of Norwood's commercial center had been realized. This view of Washington Street approaching Cottage Street and the town common shows a radical change from the sleepy village atmosphere of the area known as the "Hook."

The Sanborn Block is named for George Edward Sanborn, who was born in South Dedham in 1870. He acquired the hardware business of E.W. Talbot in 1891. In 1907, the Sanborn Block was erected on the west side of Washington Street between Day and Vernon Streets.

In 1927, Thomas A. Hayden and William C. Breen opened the Norwood Theater on the east side of Central Street opposite the town common. South Norwood's New South Theater at 1182 Washington Street was opened in 1913. The Premier Theater near the Washington and Guild Street intersection was renamed the Guild Theater when Norwood architect William G. Upham extensively remodeled it in the early 1930s. Upham also designed the Norwood Theater, the Norwood Town Hall, and the 1935 Norwood Post Office.

Motion pictures came to Norwood in 1907. These early motion pictures were screened in Village Hall and in a tent pitched at Cottage and Washington Streets. In 1910, Charles Hubbard opened the Premier Theater (later renamed the Guild Theater) on the east side of Washington Street between Day and Guild Streets.

This *c.* 1921 photograph shows Norwood's Railroad Avenue looking west as it intersects with Washington Street. The opposite direction leads to Norwood's "Cork City" neighborhood.

This was the Norwood Trust Company float used in the Norwood NRA parade of October 19, 1933. The Norwood Trust Company was the original bank to occupy the northwest corner of Day and Washington Streets.

This peaceful view of a traffic-free Dean Street in South Norwood as it proceeds east shows an area that is quite different from the congested crossroads here in 1997. The railroad bridge constructed in 1891 can be seen in the distance.

The commercial gateway to South Norwood is shown here at the intersection of Washington Street and Dean Street. At the turn of the twentieth century, South Norwood experienced a spurt in residential and business construction providing homes and jobs for the recent immigrant population boom.

The Morrill Memorial Library was presented to the town by Louise and George H. Morrill Sr. in memory of his daughter, Sarah Bond Morrill, who died of typhoid fever at the age of twenty-three. Dedicated in 1898, it was constructed in the Romanesque style with Dudlin granite from Oakland, Maine, and a red-tiled roof. Carved in the base are the names of writers. Above the windows are replicas of ancient printers' marks. South Dedham's second minister, Reverend Jabez Chickering, began the original book collection for the citizens of South Dedham. He collected ninety-three volumes for the parishioners to circulate. This collection is on display at the headquarters of the Norwood Historical Society's Day House.

Both Morrill Memorial Library and Bond Street are named in memory of Sarah Bond Morrill.

George F. Willett, Norwood's visionary and philanthropist, was born in Walpole on August 7, 1870. In 1895 he acquired a controlling interest in the Winslow Brothers Tannery founded by the ancestors of his wife, Edith Winslow. The Willett era, from 1909 to 1920, was of major importance to the growth of Norwood. Willett's broad-minded views and generous public spirit were instrumental in moving Norwood into the twentieth century. Among other contributions, he gave $500,000 for the funding of the Norwood Hospital, and for the acquisition of the land in the former Hook area for a town common. This was the beginning of the modernization of Washington Street. In 1914, Willett was credited with conceiving the idea of a town manager to conduct the business of the town.

Edith Winslow Willett (1872–1943) was the daughter of South Dedham/Norwood's nineteenth-century civic leader F.O. Winslow, and was the wife of George Willett, Norwood's twentieth-century civic leader.

An estimated 25,000 people on Sunday, May 9, 1943, paid tribute to Norwood's six Gold Star Mothers and some 1,400 Norwood men in the service, as Governor Leverett Saltonstall delivered an inspiring address at the unveiling of the Norwood Honor Roll on the town green.

A huge eighty-two-unit parade preceded the dedication with fourteen bands supplying martial music along the line of march. (Article from the *Norwood Daily Messenger*, May 12, 1943.)

The Norwood Civic Association was partially destroyed by fire on April 22, 1930. Four buildings valued at $100,000 were destroyed in this fire. Only the social hall and swimming pool were saved. The remaining buildings were demolished in 1981. The Civic occupied the east side of Washington Street between East Hoyle and Winter Streets.

A familiar U.S. Route 1 site in Norwood was the Neponset Valley Farm Ice Cream stand on the southbound side. Passers-by recall the sight of dairy cows grazing on the hillside adjacent to the ice cream stand, well into the 1960s.

Ten
Community Spirit

The Norwood Brass Band, formed in 1866, poses in front of the Universalist Church on Washington Street. The band built its own hall in 1891 and held summer evening concerts at the town's original bandstand, which was located in Guild Square.

This familiar Norwood bandstand was located in Guild Square across from the post office.

Police Chief James Lavers leads a Memorial Day parade along Washington Street on the way to the Old Cemetery, *c.* 1912.

Norwood's YMCA chapter was organized in 1892. The chapter met in the Morrill Block building on Washington Street.

Members of Norwood's George K. Bird Post, Grand Army of the Republic (GAR), chartered in 1884, met at Village Hall on Washington Street. The GAR was the veterans' organization for those who served in the Union Army during the War between the States. The photograph dates from about 1890.

Raphael "Rafe" Hoyle was a printer and cycling enthusiast. The road leading to his family's farm became Norwood's Hoyle Street. He died in 1928.

This July 4, 1895 gathering at George S. Winslow's home on Walpole Street included much of the "who's who" of Norwood—Morrill, Shattuck, Plimpton, Smith, Lane, and other well-known "townies."

Norwood-born Ernest W. "Pete" Ellis, age twenty, was the change pitcher for the Manchester, New Hampshire, Independent Baseball Club in 1886. Note the flower-draped bat he is holding.

Norwood's first baseball team, organized in 1874, was made up of young men working for Tyler Thayer's construction business. By the time of this 1908 photograph of Norwood High School's team, baseball was a popular sport in town.

A Norwood High School girls' basketball team, *c.* 1900, uses a tall ladder to pose for their team picture.

The Great Bar-None Circus comes to Norwood *c.* 1885. The photograph shows the west side of Washington Street between Cottage and Nahatan Streets.

Celebrating "Old Home Week" in 1903, these people posed for a photograph on the north side of the Lyman Smith house when it was located on Washington Street. The house was relocated to 15 Vernon Street in 1915.

Prospect Park, located at the southeast corner of Vernon and Prospect Streets, was the scene of Norwood's football and baseball games in 1902.

Canoeing on Norwood's Ellis Pond was a popular activity in the 1890s. Before the Ellis brothers succeeded in marketing ice from the pond, its water was used to power a wrapping paper mill founded by Isaac Ellis in 1832. "Ellis Pond water is pure," wrote the *Norwood Messenger* in 1932, "but clean ice is no accident. Each fall the water is allowed to run as low as is safely possible and the entire shore is cleaned of rubbish and leaves."

In a peaceful moment Otis Baker, about eight years old in 1896, enjoyed the country life along Hawes Brook. A patient photographer focused with great clarity on the little sailboat, recording the scene with an artist's sense of composition. The boathouse at Ellis Pond can be seen on the dam upstream.

By June 1933 the U.S. Congress had voted to amend the constitution repealing Prohibition.
The lengthy process of ratification by the forty-eight states was underway. These friends

C. — ELLIS GROVE — NORWOOD JUNE, 1933

gathered, a little prematurely, to celebrate the repeal and the end of Prohibition, which was ratified by the states in December 1933.

These boys are riding on Beacon Street toward Bullard Street and the Beacon School, which was located to the rear of today's Morrill Memorial Library. Dr. Francis Cragin's house is on the right.

Men in costumes parade up Washington Street carrying a banner reading, "The New Improved Steamer No. 190—the Long Felt Want of Norwood." The house in the background is the Lyman Smith house at its original location on the northwest corner of Washington and Vernon Streets.